I0439126

Informing the legislative debate since 1914 _____

Broadband Loan and Grant Programs in the USDA's Rural Utilities Service

Lennard G. Kruger
Specialist in Science and Technology Policy

June 23, 2014

Congressional Research Service

7-5700

www.crs.gov

RL33816

Summary

Given the large potential impact broadband access may have on the economic development of rural America, concern has been raised over a "digital divide" between rural and urban or suburban areas with respect to broadband deployment. While there are many examples of rural communities with state of the art telecommunications facilities, recent surveys and studies have indicated that, in general, rural areas tend to lag behind urban and suburban areas in broadband deployment.

Citing the lagging deployment of broadband in many rural areas, Congress and the Administration acted in 2001 and 2002 to initiate pilot broadband loan and grant programs within the Rural Utilities Service (RUS) at the U.S. Department of Agriculture (USDA). Subsequently, Section 6103 of the Farm Security and Rural Investment Act of 2002 (P.L. 107-171) amended the Rural Electrification Act of 1936 to authorize a loan and loan guarantee program to provide funds for the costs of the construction, improvement, and acquisition of facilities and equipment for broadband service in eligible rural communities. The RUS/USDA houses two assistance programs exclusively dedicated to financing broadband deployment: the Rural Broadband Access Loan and Loan Guarantee Program and the Community Connect Grant Program.

The 110th Congress considered reauthorization and modification of the loan and loan guarantee program as part of the 2008 farm bill. The Food, Conservation, and Energy Act of 2008 became law on June 18, 2008 (P.L. 110-246). Title VI (Rural Development) contains authorizing language for the broadband loan program.

In the 113th Congress, the 2014 farm bill (P.L. 113-79, the Agricultural Act of 2014) was signed by the President on February 7, 2014. P.L. 113-79 amends Section 601 of the Rural Electrification Act of 1936 (7 U.S.C. 950bb) to reauthorize the Rural Broadband Access Loan and Loan Guarantee Program through FY2018. P.L. 113-79 also includes provisions to redefine project area eligibility with respect to existing broadband service, increase the program's transparency and reporting requirements, define a minimum level of broadband service, require a study on the gathering and use of address-level data, and establish a new Rural Gigabit Network Pilot Program.

Contents

Tables

Contacts

Background: Broadband and Rural America

The broadband loan and grant programs at RUS are intended to accelerate the deployment of broadband services in rural America. "Broadband" refers to high-speed Internet access and advanced telecommunications services for private homes, commercial establishments, schools, and public institutions. Currently in the United States, residential broadband is primarily provided via mobile wireless (e.g., smartphones), cable modem (from the local provider of cable television service), or over the telephone line (digital subscriber line or "DSL"). Other broadband technologies include fiber optic cable, fixed wireless, satellite, and broadband over power lines (BPL).

Broadband access enables a number of beneficial applications to individual users and to communities. These include e-commerce, telecommuting, voice service (voice over the Internet protocol or "VOIP"), distance learning, telemedicine, public safety, and others. It is becoming generally accepted that broadband access in a community can play an important role in economic development. A February 2006 study by the Massachusetts Institute of Technology for the Department of Commerce's Economic Development Administration marked the first attempt to measure the impact of broadband on economic growth. The study found that "between 1998 and 2002, communities in which mass-market broadband was available by December 1999 experienced more rapid growth in employment, the number of businesses overall, and businesses in IT-intensive sectors, relative to comparable communities without broadband at that time."[1]

Subsequently, a June 2007 report from the Brookings Institution found that for every one percentage point increase in broadband penetration in a state, employment is projected to increase by 0.2% to 0.3% per year. For the entire U.S. private non-farm economy, the study projected an increase of about 300,000 jobs, assuming the economy is not already at full employment.[2] Similarly, an August 2009 report from the USDA Economic Research Service found that counties with a longer history of broadband availability had higher employment growth and higher nonfarm private earnings than similarly situated counties with little or no broadband access since 2000.[3]

Access to affordable broadband is viewed as particularly important for the economic development of rural areas because it enables individuals and businesses to participate fully in the online economy regardless of geographical location. For example, aside from enabling existing businesses to remain in their rural locations, broadband access could attract new business enterprises drawn by lower costs and a more desirable lifestyle. Essentially, broadband potentially allows businesses and individuals in rural America to live locally while competing globally in an online environment.

---

[1] Gillett, Sharon E., Massachusetts Institute of Technology, *Measuring Broadband's Economic Impact*, report prepared for the Economic Development Administration, U.S. Department of Commerce, February 28, 2006, p. 4, available at http://www.eda.gov/ImageCache/EDAPublic/documents/pdfdocs2006/mitcmubbimpactreport_2epdf/v1/mitcmubbimpactreport.pdf.

[2] Crandall, Robert, William Lehr, and Robert Litan, *The Effects of Broadband Deployment on Output and Employment: A Cross-sectional Analysis of U.S. Data*, June 2007, 20 pp., http://www3.brookings.edu/views/papers/crandall/200706litan.pdf.

[3] Peter Stenberg, Mitchell Morehart, and Stephen Vogel, et al., *Broadband Internet's Value for Rural America*, United States Department of Agriculture, Economic Research Service, Economic Research Report Number 78, Washington, DC, August 2009, p. iii, http://www.ers.usda.gov/Publications/ERR78/ERR78.pdf.

Given the large potential impact broadband may have on the economic development of rural America, concern has been raised over a "digital divide" between rural and urban or suburban areas with respect to broadband deployment. While there are many examples of rural communities with state of the art telecommunications facilities,[4] recent surveys and studies have indicated that, in general, rural areas tend to lag behind urban and suburban areas in broadband deployment. For example:

- According to 2013 survey data from the Pew Research Center, 70% of adults in urban areas said they have a high-speed broadband connection at home, as opposed to 62% of adults in rural areas.[5]

- A study commissioned by the National Agricultural & Rural Development Policy Center noted a persistent 13 percentage point gap in broadband adoption between metropolitan and non-metropolitan areas between 2003 and 2010.[6]

- The Department of Commerce report, *Exploring the Digital Nation: America's Emerging Online Experience*, found that while the digital divide between urban and rural areas has lessened since 2007, it still persists with 72% of urban households adopting broadband service in 2011, compared to 58% of rural households.[7]

- According to June 2013 data from the National Broadband Map, 99.9% of the population in urban areas have access to available broadband download speeds of at least 6 Mbps, as opposed to 91.7% of the population in rural areas.[8]

The comparatively lower population density of rural areas is likely the major reason why broadband is less deployed than in more highly populated suburban and urban areas. Particularly for wireline broadband technologies—such as cable modem, fiber, and DSL—the greater the geographical distances among customers, the larger the cost to serve those customers. Thus, there is often less incentive for companies to invest in broadband in rural areas than, for example, in an urban area where there is more demand (more customers with perhaps higher incomes) and less cost to wire the market area.

The terrain of rural areas can also be a hindrance, in that it is more expensive to deploy broadband technologies in a mountainous or heavily forested area. An additional added cost factor for remote areas can be the expense of "backhaul" (e.g., the "middle mile") which refers to the installation of a dedicated line which transmits a signal to and from an Internet backbone which is typically located in or near an urban area.

---

[4] See for example: National Exchange Carrier Association (NECA), *Trends 2010: A Report on Rural Telecom Technology*, 23 p., https://www.neca.org/cms400min/WorkArea/DownloadAsset.aspx?id=4892.

[5] *Home Broadband 2013*, p. 3.

[6] Brian Whiteacre, Roberto Gallardo, and Sharon Strover, National Agricultural & Rural Development Policy Center, *Rural Broadband Availability and Adoption: Evidence, Policy Challenges, and Options*, March 2013, p. 13, available at http://www.nardep.info/Broadband_2.html.

[7] U.S. Department of Commerce, National Telecommunications and Information Administration, *Exploring the Digital Nation: America's Emerging Online Experience*, June 2013, p. 26, available at http://www.ntia.doc.gov/files/ntia/publications/exploring_the_digital_nation_-_americas_emerging_online_experience.pdf.

[8] NTIA, National Broadband Map, *Broadband Statistics Report: Broadband Availability in Urban vs. Rural Areas*, February 2014, p. 7, available at http://www.broadbandmap.gov/download/Broadband%20Availability%20in%20Rural%20vs%20Urban%20Areas.pdf.

Pilot Broadband Loan and Grant Programs

Given the lagging deployment of broadband in rural areas, Congress and the Administration acted to initiate pilot broadband loan and grant programs within the Rural Utilities Service of the U.S. Department of Agriculture. While RUS had long maintained telecommunications loan and grant programs (Rural Telephone Loans and Loan Guarantees, Rural Telephone Bank, and more recently, the Distance Learning and Telemedicine Loans and Grants) none were exclusively dedicated to financing rural broadband deployment. Title III of the FY2001 agriculture appropriations bill (P.L. 106-387) directed USDA/RUS to conduct a "pilot program to finance broadband transmission and local dial-up Internet service in areas that meet the definition of 'rural area' used for the Distance Learning and Telemedicine Program."

Subsequently, on December 5, 2000, RUS announced the availability of $100 million in loan funding through a one-year pilot program "to finance the construction and installation of broadband telecommunications services in rural America."[9] The broadband pilot loan program was authorized under the authority of the Distance Learning and Telemedicine Program (7 U.S.C. 950aaa), and was available to "legally organized entities" not located within the boundaries of a city or town having a population in excess of 20,000.

The FY2001 pilot broadband loan program received applications requesting a total of $350 million. RUS approved funding for 12 applications totaling $100 million. The FY2002 agriculture appropriations bill (P.L. 107-76) designated a loan level of $80 million for broadband loans, and on January 23, 2002, RUS announced that the pilot program would be extended into FY2002, with $80 million in loans made available to fund many of the applications that did not receive funding during the previous year.[10]

Meanwhile, the FY2002 agriculture appropriations bill (P.L. 107-76) allocated $20 million for a pilot broadband grant program, also authorized under the Distance Learning and Telemedicine Program. On July 8, 2002, RUS announced the availability of $20 million for a pilot grant program for the provision of broadband service in rural America. The program was specifically targeted to economically challenged rural communities with no existing broadband service. Grants were made available to entities providing "community-oriented connectivity," which the RUS defined as those entities "who will connect the critical community facilities including the local schools, libraries, hospitals, police, fire and rescue services and who will operate a community center that provides free and open access to residents."[11]

In response to the July 8, 2002, Notice of Funds Availability, RUS received more than 300 applications totaling more than $185 million in requested grant funding. RUS approved 40 grants totaling $20 million. The pilot program was extended into FY2003, as the Consolidated Appropriations Resolution of 2003 (P.L. 108-7) allocated $10 million for broadband grants. On September 24, 2003, 34 grants were awarded to eligible applicants who did not receive funding during the previous year.

---

[9] Rural Utilities Service, USDA, "Construction and Installation of Broadband Telecommunications Services in Rural America; Availability of Loan Funds," *Federal Register*, Vol. 65, No. 234, December 5, 2000, p. 75920.

[10] Rural Utilities Service, USDA, "Broadband Pilot Loan Program," *Federal Register*, Vol. 67, No. 15, January 23, 2002, p. 3140.

[11] Rural Utilities Service, USDA, "Broadband Pilot Grant Program," *Federal Register*, Vol. 67, No. 130, July 8, 2002, p. 45080.

Rural Broadband Access Loan and Loan Guarantee Program

Building on the pilot broadband loan program at RUS, Section 6103 of the Farm Security and Rural Investment Act of 2002 (P.L. 107-171) amended the Rural Electrification Act of 1936 to authorize a loan and loan guarantee program to provide funds for the costs of the construction, improvement, and acquisition of facilities and equipment for broadband service in eligible rural communities.[12] Section 6103 made available, from the funds of the Commodity Credit Corporation (CCC), a total of $100 million through FY2007. P.L. 107-171 also authorized any other funds appropriated for the broadband loan program. The program was subsequently reauthorized by Section 6110 of the Food, Conservation, and Energy Act of 2008 (P.L. 110-246), and by Section 6104 of the Agricultural Act of 2014 (P.L. 113-79).

Beginning in FY2004, Congress annually blocked mandatory funding from the CCC. Thus— starting in FY2004—the program was funded as part of annual appropriations in the Distance Learning and Telemedicine account within the Department of Agriculture appropriations bill. Every fiscal year, Congress approves an appropriation (loan subsidy) and a specific loan level (lending authority) for the Rural Broadband Access Loan and Loan Guarantee Program. **Table 1** shows—for the life of the program to date—loan subsidies and loan levels (lending authority) set by Congress in annual appropriations bills.

---

[12] Title VI of the Rural Electrification Act of 1936 (7 U.S.C. 950bb).

Table 1. Appropriations Funding for the Rural Broadband Access Loan and Loan Guarantee Program

	Direct Appropriations (subsidy level)	Loan Levels Estimated in Annual Appropriations[a]
FY2001 (pilot)	—	$100 million
FY2002 (pilot)	—	$80 million
FY2003	[b]	$80 million
FY2004	$13.1 million	$602 million
FY2005	$11.715 million	$550 million
FY2006	$10.75 million	$500 million
FY2007	$10.75 million	$500 million
FY2008	$6.45 million	$300 million
FY2009	$15.619 million	$400 million
FY2010	$28.96 million	$400 million
FY2011	$22.32 million	$400 million
FY2012	$6.0 million	$212 million
FY2013	$4 million[c]	$42 million
FY2014	$4.5 million	$34.5 million

Source: Compiled by CRS from appropriations bills.

a. Actual loan levels for a fiscal year can vary from what is estimated in annual appropriations bill.

b. Program received $40 million composed of $20 million from FY2002 plus $20 million from FY2003 of mandatory funding from the Commodity Credit Corporation, as directed by P.L. 107-171. In the FY2004, FY2005, and FY2006 appropriations bills, mandatory funding from the CCC was canceled.

c. Consolidated and Further Continuing Appropriations Act, 2013 (P.L. 113-6). Does not reflect reductions due to sequestration.

The Rural Broadband Access Loan and Loan Guarantee Program is codified as 7 U.S.C. 950bb. On February 6, 2013, the RUS published in the *Federal Register* the rule (7 C.F.R. part 1738) implementing the Rural Broadband Access Loan and Loan Guarantee Program, as reauthorized by the 2008 farm bill (P.L. 110-246).[13] Entities eligible to receive loans included corporations, limited liability companies, cooperative or mutual organizations, Indian tribes, and state or local government. Individuals or partnerships are not eligible.

Pursuant to the enactment of the Agricultural Act of 2014 (P.L. 113-79), RUS is currently developing new regulations and rules for the program. Further information is available at http://www.rurdev.usda.gov/utp_farmbill.html.

---

[13] Department of Agriculture, Rural Utilities Service, "Rural Broadband Access Loans and Loan Guarantees," 78 *Federal Register* 8353-8360, February 6, 2013, available at http://www.gpo.gov/fdsys/pkg/FR-2013-02-06/pdf/2013-02390.pdf. The final rule substantially adopts the interim rule published on March 14, 2011, available at http://www.gpo.gov/fdsys/pkg/FR-2011-03-14/pdf/2011-5615.pdf.

Community Connect Broadband Grants

The Consolidated Appropriations Act of 2004 (P.L. 108-199) appropriated $9 million "for a grant program to finance broadband transmission in rural areas eligible for Distance Learning and Telemedicine Program benefits authorized by 7 U.S.C. 950aaa." Essentially operating the same as the pilot broadband grants, the program provides grant money to applicants proposing to provide broadband on a "community-oriented connectivity" basis to currently unserved rural areas for the purpose of fostering economic growth and delivering enhanced health care, education, and public safety services. Funding for the broadband grant program is provided through annual appropriations in the Distance Learning and Telemedicine account within the Department of Agriculture appropriations bill. **Table 2** shows a history of appropriations for the Community Connect Broadband Grants.

Table 2. Appropriations for the Community Connect Broadband Grants

Fiscal Year	Appropriation
FY2002	$20 million
FY2003	$10 million
FY2004	$9 million
FY2005	$9 million
FY2006	$9 million
FY2007	$9 million
FY2008	$13.4 million
FY2009	$13.4 million
FY2010	$17.9 million
FY2011	$13.4 million
FY2012	$10.4 million
FY2013	$10.4 million[a]
FY2014	$10.4 million

Source: Compiled by CRS from appropriations bills.

a. Consolidated and Further Continuing Appropriations Act, 2013 (P.L. 113-6). Does not reflect reductions due to sequestration.

Eligible applicants for broadband grants include incorporated organizations, Indian tribes or tribal organizations, state or local units of government, or cooperatives, private corporations, and limited liability companies organized on a for profit or not-for-profit basis. Individuals or partnerships are not eligible.

Funded projects must serve a rural area where broadband service does not exist, deploy free basic broadband service for at least two years to all community facilities, offer basic broadband to residential and business customers, and provide a community center with at least 10 computer access points within the proposed service area while making broadband available for two years at no charge to users within that community center.

On May 3, 2013, RUS issued a new final rule for Community Connect grants in the *Federal Register*.[14] The final rule changes previous requirements related to matching funds, eligible communities, and application scoring criteria. The final rule also removes the previous definition of broadband service speed (200 kbps). A new threshold for broadband service speed and broadband grant speed (the speed the grantee must deliver) will be provided in an annual Notice of Funding Availability (NOFA) in the *Federal Register*. The NOFA will also specify the deadline for applications, the total amount of funding available, and the maximum and minimum amount of funding available for each grant. Further information, including application materials and guidelines, is available at http://www.rurdev.usda.gov/utp_commconnect.html.

The American Recovery and Reinvestment Act (P.L. 111-5)

On February 17, 2009, President Obama signed P.L. 111-5, the American Recovery and Reinvestment Act (ARRA). Broadband provisions of the ARRA provided a total of $7.2 billion, primarily for broadband grants. The total consisted of $2.5 billion to RUS broadband loan, grant, and loan/grant combinations, and $4.7 billion to NTIA/DOC for a newly established Broadband Technology Opportunities Program.[15]

The ARRA did not specify how the $2.5 billion is to be divided between the RUS grant and loan programs. Regarding projects applying for funding, the ARRA stated that

- at least 75% of the area to be served by a project receiving these funds shall be in a rural area without sufficient access to high speed broadband service to facilitate economic development, as determined by the Secretary of Agriculture;

- priority shall be given to projects that will deliver end users a choice of more than one broadband service provider;

- priority shall be given to projects that provide service to the highest proportion of rural residents that do not have access to broadband service;

- priority shall be given to borrowers and former borrowers of rural telephone loans;

- priority shall be given to projects demonstrating that all project elements will be fully funded, that can commence promptly, and that can be completed; and

- no area of a project may receive funding to provide broadband service under the Broadband Technology Opportunities Program at NTIA/DOC.

The ARRA also directed the Federal Communications Commission to develop a National Broadband Plan (NBP). The NBP was released on March 16, 2010. Among its many recommendations, the FCC recommended that Congress should consider expanding combination

---

[14] Department of Agriculture, Rural Utilities Service, "Community Connect Broadband Grant Program," 78 *Federal Register* 25787-25795, May 3, 2013, available at http://www.gpo.gov/fdsys/pkg/FR-2013-05-03/pdf/2013-10502.pdf.

[15] For more information on ARRA broadband programs, see CRS Report R41775, *Background and Issues for Congressional Oversight of ARRA Broadband Awards*, by Lennard G. Kruger.

grant-loan programs. The NBP also recommended that Congress should consider expanding the Community Connect grant program, both in size and in the scope of its eligibility criteria.

Impact of Universal Service Reform on RUS Broadband Loan Programs

RUS currently has three programs that provide loans for broadband infrastructure projects: the Rural Broadband Access Loan and Loan Guarantee program (also known as the Farm Bill broadband loan program), the Broadband Initiatives Program (BIP under the ARRA), and the Telecommunications Infrastructure Loan Program (established in 1949 as the Rural Telephone Loan and Loan Guarantee program).[16]

Whereas RUS broadband loans are used as up-front capital to invest in broadband infrastructure, the Federal Communications Commission's (FCC's) Universal Service Fund (USF)—specifically, the high cost fund—has functioned as an ongoing subsidy to keep the operation of telecommunications networks in high cost areas profitable for providers. Many RUS telecommunications and broadband borrowers (loan recipients) receive high cost USF subsidies. In many cases, the subsidy received from USF helps provide the revenue necessary to keep the loan viable. The Telecommunications Infrastructure Loan Program is highly dependent on high cost USF revenues, with 99% (476 out of 480 borrowers) receiving interstate high cost USF support. This is not surprising, given that the RUS Telecommunications Infrastructure Loans are available only to the most rural and high cost areas (towns with populations less than 5,000). Regarding broadband loans, 60% of BIP (stimulus) borrowers draw from state or interstate USF support mechanisms, while 10% of Farm Bill (Rural Broadband Access Loan and Loan Guarantee Program) broadband borrowers receive interstate high cost USF support.[17]

The FCC, in an October 2011 decision, adopted an order that calls for the USF to be transformed, in stages, over a multi-year period—from a mechanism to support voice telephone service to one that supports the deployment, adoption, and use of both fixed and mobile broadband. More specifically, the high cost program is being phased out and a new fund, the Connect America Fund (CAF), which includes the targeted Mobility Fund and new Remote Areas Fund, is replacing it.[18]

During this transition, the uncertainty surrounding the FCC's proposed methodology for distributing Connect America Fund monies has led many small rural providers to postpone or cancel investment in broadband network upgrades.[19] According to RUS, "demand for RUS loans

---

[16] For more information on the RUS portfolio of telecommunications and broadband programs offering loans, loan guarantees, grants, and loan/grant combinations, see CRS Report R42524, *Rural Broadband: The Roles of the Rural Utilities Service and the Universal Service Fund*, by Angele A. Gilroy and Lennard G. Kruger.

[17] Jessica Zufolo, Deputy Administrator, RUS, *Overview of the RUS Telecommunications Loan and Grant Programs*, July 2011, Slide 7, http://www.narucmeetings.org/Presentations/Zufolo_7-2011.pdf.

[18] For more information, see CRS Report R42524, *Rural Broadband: The Roles of the Rural Utilities Service and the Universal Service Fund*, by Angele A. Gilroy and Lennard G. Kruger.

[19] According to a January 2013 survey conducted by NTCA—The Rural Broadband Association, 69% of member companies responding to the survey had either cancelled or postponed $492.7 million in broadband investments due to the uncertainty surrounding the transition to the FCC's Connect America Fund. See NTCA—The Rural Broadband Association, *Survey: FCC USF/ICC Impacts*, January 2013, available at http://www.ntca.org/images/stories/ (continued...)

---

dropped to roughly 37% of the total amount of loan funds appropriated by Congress in FY2012," and that "[c]urrent and prospective RUS borrowers have communicated their hesitation to increase their outstanding debt and move forward with planned construction due to the recently implemented reductions in USF support and Inter-Carrier Compensation (ICC) payments."[20]

Appropriations

The Rural Broadband Access Loan and Loan Guarantee Program and the Community Connect Grant Program are funded through the annual Agriculture, Rural Development, Food and Drug Administration, and Related Agencies Appropriations Act. The appropriation provided to the broadband loan program is a loan subsidy which supports a significantly higher loan level.

Table 3. Recent and Proposed Appropriations for RUS Broadband Programs

(dollars)

	FY2013 (P.L. 113-6)	FY2014 (Admin. Request)	FY2014 (P.L. 113-76)	FY2015 (Admin. Request)	FY2015 (H.Rept. 113-468)	FY2015 (S.Rept. 113-164)
Broadband Loans	4.0 million (42 million loan level)	8.3 million (63 million loan level)	4.5 million (34.5 million loan level)	8.3 million (44.2 million loan level)	4.5 million (24.1 million loan level)	6.4 million (34.4 million loan level)
Community Connect Grants	10.372 million	10.372 million	10.372 million	20.372 million	10.372 million	10.372 million

FY2012

The Administration's FY2012 budget proposal requested no funding for the Rural Broadband Access Loan and Loan Guarantee Program, citing an anticipated accumulation of past-year unobligated funding that would support a loan level totaling $1.2 billion. Since the FY2012 budget proposal was released, however, the Department of Defense and Full-Year Continuing Appropriations Act, 2011 (P.L. 112-10) rescinded all available unobligated budget authority from past years.

The Administration's FY2012 budget proposal requested $18 million for the Community Connect Grant Program.

On June 3, 2011, the House Appropriations Committee reported H.R. 2112, the Agriculture, Rural Development, Food and Drug Administration, and Related Agencies Appropriations Act, 2012. As reported (H.Rept. 112-101), H.R. 2112 would provide no funding for either the Rural Broadband Access Loan and Loan Guarantee Program or the Community Connect Grant Program. On June 16, 2011, the House approved (by a vote of 221-198) an amendment offered by

---

(...continued)

Documents/Advocacy/SurveyReports/FCC_USF_ICC_ImpactSurvey.pdf.

[20] Letter from RUS to the FCC, February 13, 2013, available at https://prodnet.www neca.org/publicationsdocs/wwpdf/ 21513usda.pdf.

Representative Gibson that provides $6 million in budget authority for the broadband loan program. H.R. 2112, passed by the House on June 16, 2011, would provide a loan level of $210 million.

On September 7, 2011, the Senate Appropriations Committee reported its version of H.R. 2112 (S.Rept. 112-73). The Senate mark would provide $8 million in budget authority for broadband loans and a loan level of $282 million. The committee also provided $10.372 million for Community Connect grants. In its bill report, the committee encourages RUS to focus expenditures on projects that bring broadband service to currently unserved households.

On November 18, 2011, the President signed the Consolidated and Further Continuing Appropriations Act, 2012 (P.L. 112-55). P.L. 112-55 includes the conference agreement levels for RUS broadband programs, including $6 million for the broadband loan program (subsidizing a loan level of $212 million) and $10.372 million for Community Connect grants. The conference report (H.Rept. 112-284) states that broadband funding is "intended to promote broadband availability in those areas where there is not otherwise a business case for private investment in a broadband network." The conferees encourage RUS to focus expenditures on "projects that bring broadband service to currently unserved households."

FY2013

The Administration's FY2013 budget proposal requested $8.915 million to subsidize a loan level of $94.139 million. The loan level is a reduction of $75 million from what was available in FY2012 ($169 million). According to the budget proposal, the reduction "will provide a program level that is consistent with historical annual demand for this program." The increase in loan subsidy (from $6 million in FY2012 to $8.915 million in FY2013) is due to an increase in the program subsidy rate that is caused by an increase in actual defaults in the program.

The Administration requested $13.379 million for broadband Community Connect grants, which is a $3 million increase over the FY2012 level.

On April 26, 2012, the Senate Appropriations Committee reported S. 2375, the Agriculture, Rural Development, Food and Drug Administration, and Related Agencies Appropriations Bill, 2013. For FY2013, the committee recommended an appropriation of $6 million to subsidize a loan level of $63 million for the broadband loan and loan guarantee program. The committee recommended $10.372 million for broadband grants. In the bill report (S.Rept. 112-163), the committee stated that funds for the broadband program are intended to promote broadband availability in those areas where there is not otherwise a business case for private investment in a broadband network. The committee encouraged RUS to focus on projects that bring broadband to currently unserved households.

On June 19, 2012, the House Appropriations Committee reported its version of the agriculture appropriations bill, H.R. 5973. The committee recommended an appropriation of $2 million to subsidize a loan level of $21 million for the broadband loan and loan guarantee program. The committee recommended $10.165 million for broadband grants. In the bill report (H.Rept. 112-542), the committee stated that funds for the broadband program are intended to promote broadband availability in those areas where there is not otherwise a business case for private investment in a broadband network, and directed RUS to focus expenditures on projects that bring broadband to currently unserved households. Additionally, the committee expressed concern and disappointment with the progress of RUS broadband projects funded by the

American Recovery and Reinvestment Act (ARRA). The committee also directed USDA to prepare reports on how the FCC's Universal Service Fund and Intercarrier Compensation reforms are likely to affect RUS telecommunications borrowers.

The Consolidated and Further Continuing Appropriations Act, 2013 (P.L. 113-6) funds the broadband loan program at $4 million (supporting a loan level of approximately $42 million) and the Community Connect grant program is funded at $10.372 million.

FY2014

The Administration's FY2014 budget proposal requested $8.268 million to subsidize a broadband loan level of $63.356 million. According to the budget proposal, a greater subsidy amount is needed in FY2014 "due to an increase in the cumulative principal write-off rate for this program, causing the subsidy rate to increase from 9.47 percent in 2013 to 13.05 percent in 2014." The Administration requested $10.372 million for the Community Connect grant program.

On June 13, 2013, the House Appropriations Committee approved the FY2014 Agriculture Appropriations Act (H.R. 2410, H.Rept. 113-116). The bill provides $5.5 million to subsidize a loan level of $42.146 million for the broadband loan program, and $10.111 million for the Community Connect grant program. In the bill report, the committee states that funding provided for the broadband program is intended to promote broadband availability in those areas where there is not otherwise a business case for private investment in a broadband network. The committee directs RUS to focus expenditures on projects that bring broadband service to currently unserved households.

On June 20, 2013, the Senate Appropriations Committee approved its version of the FY2014 Agriculture Appropriations Act (S. 1244, S.Rept. 113-46). The bill provides $4 million to subsidize a loan level of $30.651 million for the broadband loan program, and $10.372 million for the Community Connect grant program.

The Consolidated Appropriations Act, 2014 (P.L. 113-76) funds the broadband loan program at $4.5 million (supporting a loan level of $34.5 million), and the Community Connect grant program is funded at $10.372 million.

FY2015

The Administration's FY2015 budget proposal requested $8.268 million to subsidize a broadband loan level of $44.238 million. For the Community Connect grant program, the Administration requested $20.372 million, which is about double the FY2014 level.

On May 29, 2014, the House Appropriations Committee approved the FY2015 Agriculture Appropriations Act (H.R. 4800, H.Rept. 113-468). The bill provides $4.5 million to subsidize a loan level of $24.077 million for the broadband loan program, and $10.372 million for the Community Connect grant program. According to the bill report, priority for the broadband loan program is to promote broadband availability in those areas where there is not otherwise a business case for private investment in a broadband network. RUS is directed to focus on projects that bring broadband service to currently unserved households.

On May 22, 2014, the Senate Appropriations Committee approved its version of the FY2015 Agriculture Appropriations Act (S. 2389, S.Rept. 113-164). The bill provides $6.435 million to subsidize a loan level of $34.430 million for the broadband loan program, and $10.372 million for the Community Connect grant program. The Committee recommends that the broadband loan program promote broadband availability in those areas where there is not otherwise a business case for private investment in a broadband network, and encourages RUS to focus on projects that bring broadband service to currently unserved households.

Criticisms of RUS Broadband Programs

RUS broadband programs have been awarding funds to entities serving rural communities since FY2001. Since their inception, a number of criticisms have emerged.

Loan Approval and Application Process

Perhaps the major criticism of the broadband loan program was that not enough loans are approved, thereby making it difficult for rural communities to take full advantage of the program. As of June 22, 2009, the broadband loan program received 225 applications, requesting a total of $4.7 billion in loans. Of these, 97 applications were approved (totaling $1.8 billion), 120 were returned (totaling $2.7 billion), and 8 are pending (totaling $170 million).[21] According to RUS officials, 28% of available loan money was awarded in 2004, and only 5% of available loan money was awarded in 2005.[22]

The loan application process has been criticized as being overly complex and burdensome, requiring applicants to spend months preparing costly market research and engineering assessments. Many applications are rejected because the applicant's business plan is deemed insufficient to support a commercially viable business. The biggest reason for applications being returned has been insufficient credit support, whereby applicants do not have sufficient cash-on-hand (one year's worth is required in most cases). The requirement for cash-on-hand is viewed as particularly onerous for small startup companies, many of whom lack sufficient capital to qualify for the loan. Such companies, critics assert, may be those entities most in need of financial assistance.

In report language to the FY2006 Department of Agriculture Appropriations Act (P.L. 109-97), the Senate Appropriations Committee (S.Rept. 109-92) directed the RUS "to reduce the burdensome application process and make the program requirements more reasonable, particularly in regard to cash-on-hand requirements." The committee also directed USDA to hire more full-time employees to remedy delays in application processing times.

At a May 17, 2006, hearing held by the Senate Committee on Agriculture, Nutrition, and Forestry, the Administrator of the RUS stated that RUS is working to make the program more user friendly, while at the same time protecting taxpayer investment:

---

[21] Private communication, USDA, June 23, 2009.

[22] GAO, *Broadband Deployment is Extensive throughout the United States, but It Is Difficult to Assess the Extent of Deployment Gaps in Rural Areas*, p. 33.

> As good stewards of the taxpayers' money, we must make loans that are likely to be repaid. One of the challenges in determining whether a proposed project has a reasonable chance of success is validating the market analysis of the proposed service territory and ensuring that sufficient resources are available to cover operating expenses throughout the construction period until such a time that cash flow from operations become sufficient. The loan application process that we have developed ensures that the applicant addresses these areas and that appropriate resources are available for maintaining a viable operation.[23]

According to RUS, the loan program was initially overwhelmed by applications (particularly during a two week period in August 2003), and as the program matured, application review times have dropped.[24] On May 11, 2007, RUS released a Proposed Rule which sought to revise regulations for the broadband loan program. In the background material accompanying the Proposed Rule, RUS stated that the average application processing time in 2006 was almost half of what it was in 2003.[25]

Eligibility Criteria

Since the inception of the broadband grant and loan programs, the criteria for applicant eligibility have been criticized both for being too broad and for being too narrow. An audit report released by USDA's Office of Inspector General (IG) found that the "programs' focus has shifted away from those rural communities that would not, without Government assistance, have access to broadband technologies."[26] Specifically the IG report found that the RUS definition of rural area has been "too broad to distinguish usefully between suburban and rural communities,"[27] with the result that, as of March 10, 2005, $103.4 million in loans and grants (nearly 12% of total funding awarded) had been awarded to 64 communities located near large cities. The report cited examples of affluent suburban subdivisions qualifying as rural areas under the program guidelines and receiving broadband loans.[28]

On the other hand, eligibility requirements have also been criticized as too narrow. For example, the limitation of assistance only to communities of 20,000 or less in population excludes small rural towns that may exceed this limit, and also excludes many municipalities seeking to deploy their own networks.[29] Similarly, per capita income requirements can preclude higher income communities with higher costs of living (e.g., rural Alaska), and the limitation of grant programs

---

[23] Testimony of Jim Andrew, Administrator, Rural Utilities Service, U.S. Department of Agriculture, "Broadband Program Administered by USDA's Rural Utilities Service," full committee hearing before the Senate Committee on Agriculture, Nutrition, and Forestry, 109th Congress, May 17, 2006.

[24] Rural Utilities Service, private communication, January 18, 2007.

[25] Rural Utilities Service, Department of Agriculture, "Rural Broadband Access Loans and Loan Guarantees," Proposed Rule, *Federal Register*, Vol. 72, No. 91, May 11, 2007, p. 26744.

[26] U.S. Department of Agriculture, Office of Inspector General, Southwest Region, *Audit Report: Rural Utilities Service Broadband Grant and Loan Programs*, Audit Report 09601-4-Te, September 2005, p. I, http://www.usda.gov/oig/webdocs/09601-04-TE.pdf.

[27] Ibid., p. 6.

[28] Ibid., p. 8.

[29] Martinez, Michael, "Broadband: Loan Fund's Strict Rules Foil Small Municipalities," *National Journal's Technology Daily*, August 23, 2005.

only to underserved areas excludes rural communities with existing but very limited broadband access.[30]

Loans to Communities With Existing Providers

The IG report found that RUS too often has given loans to communities with existing broadband service. The IG report found that "RUS has not ensured that communities without broadband service receive first priority for loans," and that although RUS has a system in place to prioritize loans to unserved communities, the system "lacks a cutoff date and functions as a rolling selection process—priorities are decided based on the applicants who happen to be in the pool at any given moment."[31] The result is that a significant number of communities with some level of preexisting broadband service have received loans. According to the IG report, of 11 loans awarded in 2004, 66% of the associated communities served by those loans had existing service. According to RUS, 31% of communities served by all loans (during the period 2003 through early 2005) had preexisting competitive service (not including loans used to upgrade or expand existing service).[32] In some cases, according to the IG report, "loans were issued to companies in highly competitive business environments where multiple providers competed for relatively few customers."[33] At the May 1, 2007, hearing before the House Subcommittee on Specialty Crops, Rural Development, and Foreign Agriculture, then-RUS Administrator James Andrews testified that of the 69 broadband loans awarded since the program's inception, 40% of the communities approved for funding were unserved at the time of loan approval, and an additional 15% had only one broadband provider.[34]

Awarding loans to entities in communities with preexisting competitive service raised criticism from competitors who already offer broadband to those communities. According to the National Cable and Telecommunications Association (NCTA), "RUS loans are being used to unfairly subsidize second and third broadband providers in communities where private risk capital already has been invested to provide broadband service."[35] Critics argued that providing loans in areas with preexisting competitive broadband service creates an uneven playing field and discourages further private investment in rural broadband.[36] In response, RUS stated in the IG report that its policies are in accordance with the statute, and that they address "the need for competition to increase the quality of services and reduce the cost of those services to the consumer."[37] RUS argued that the presence of a competitor does not necessarily mean that an area is adequately served, and additionally, that in order for some borrowers to maintain a viable business in an

---

[30] GAO, *Broadband Deployment is Extensive throughout the United States, but It Is Difficult to Assess the Extent of Deployment Gaps in Rural Areas*, p. 33-34.

[31] Ibid., p. 13.

[32] Ibid., p. 14.

[33] Ibid., p. 15

[34] Testimony of James Andrew, Administrator, Rural Utilities Service, U.S. Department of Agriculture, before the Subcommittee on Specialty Crops, Rural Development, and Foreign Agriculture, House Committee on Agriculture, May 1, 2007.

[35] Letter from Kyle McSlarrow, President and CEO, National Cable & Telecommunications Association to the Honorable Mike Johanns, Secretary of the U.S. Department of Agriculture, May 16, 2006.

[36] Testimony of Tom Simmons, Vice President for Public Policy, Midcontinent Communications, before Senate Committee on Agriculture, Nutrition, and Forestry, May 17, 2006.

[37] *Audit Report: Rural Utilities Service Broadband Grant and Loan Programs*, p. 17.

unserved area, it may be necessary for that company to also be serving more densely populated rural areas where some level of competition already exists.[38]

Follow-Up Audit by USDA Office of Inspector General

In 2008, as directed by the House Appropriations Committee (H.Rept. 110-258, FY2008 Agriculture appropriations bill), the IG reexamined the RUS broadband loan and loan guarantee program to determine whether RUS had taken sufficient corrective actions in response to the issues raised in the 2005 IG report. The IG concluded "the key problems identified in our 2005 report—loans being issued to suburban and exurban communities and loans being issued where other providers already provide access—have not been resolved."[39]

Specifically, the follow-up IG report found that between 2005 and 2008, RUS broadband borrowers providing services in 148 communities were within 30 miles of cities with 200,000 inhabitants, including communities near very large urban areas such as Chicago and Las Vegas.

The IG report also found that since 2005 "RUS has continued providing loans to providers in markets where there is already competing service."[40] Of the 37 applications approved since September 2005, 34 loans were granted to applicants in areas where one or more private broadband providers already offered service. These 34 borrowers received $873 million to service 1,448 communities. The IG report found that since 2005, 77% of communities which were expected to receive service from a project financed by an approved RUS broadband loan had at least one existing broadband provider present, 59% had 2 or more existing providers, and 27% had 3 or more existing providers.[41]

In an official response to the follow-up IG report, RUS fundamentally disagreed with the IG criticisms, stating that the loans awarded between 2005 and 2008 were provided "in a way entirely consistent with the statutory requirements of the underlying legislation governing administration of the program, the regulations and guidance issued by the Department to implement the statute, and the intent of Congress."[42] Specifically RUS argued that its May 11, 2007, Proposed Rule, and the subsequent changes to the broadband loan and loan guarantee statute made by the 2008 farm bill, both addressed concerns over loans to non-rural areas and to communities with preexisting broadband providers. However, the Final Rule based on the Proposed Rule and the 2008 farm bill had not yet been released and implemented during the 2005-2008 period examined by the IG, and RUS was compelled by law to continue awarding broadband loans under the existing law and rules.

During 2009 and 2010, the Rural Broadband Access Loan and Loan Guarantee program was in hiatus while RUS implemented the Broadband Initiatives Program (Recovery Act grants and loans) and developed new regulations implementing the 2008 farm bill. On March 14, 2011, the new rules were released. According to Jonathan Adelstein, "this regulation and other measures

---

[38] Rural Utilities Service, private communication, January 18, 2007.

[39] U.S. Department of Agriculture, Office of Inspector General, Southwest Region, Audit Report Rural Utilities Service Broadband Loan and Loan Guarantee Program, Report No. 09601-8-Te, March 2009, p. 9.

[40] Ibid, p. 5.

[41] Ibid, p. 5-6.

[42] Ibid, p. 14.

taken by the agency have addressed all the concerns raised by the OIG," and on March 24, 2011, "the OIG notified RUS that it has closed its audits of the RUS broadband loan program."[43]

Broadband Loan Reauthorization: 2008 Farm Bill

The 110th Congress considered reauthorization of the Rural Broadband Access Loan and Loan Guarantee program as part of the 2008 farm bill. The following are some key issues which were considered during the debate over reauthorization of the RUS broadband loan and loan guarantee program.

Restricting Applicant Eligibility

The RUS broadband program was criticized for excluding too many applicants due to stringent financial requirements (e.g., the requirement that an applicant have a year's worth of cash-on-hand) and an application process—requiring detailed business plans and market surveys—that some viewed as overly expensive and burdensome to complete. During the reauthorization process, Congress considered whether the criteria for loan eligibility should be modified, and whether a more appropriate balance could be found between the need to make the program more accessible to unserved and often lower-income rural areas, and the need to protect taxpayers against bad loans.

Definition of "Rural Community"

The definition of which communities qualify as "rural" had been changed twice by statute since the broadband loan program was initiated. Under the pilot program, funds were authorized under the Distance Learning and Telemedicine Program, which defines "exceptionally rural areas" (under 5,000 inhabitants), "rural areas" (between 5,000 and 10,000) and "mid-rural areas" (between 10,000 and 20,000). RUS determined that communities of 20,000 or less would be eligible for broadband loans in cases where broadband services did not already exist.

In 2002, this definition was made narrower by the Farm Security and Rural Investment Act (P.L. 107-171), which designated eligible communities as any incorporated or unincorporated place with fewer than 20,000 inhabitants, and which was outside any standard metropolitan statistical area (MSA). The requirement that communities not be located within MSA's effectively prohibited suburban communities from receiving broadband loans. However, in 2004, the definition was again changed by the FY2004 Consolidated Appropriations Act (P.L. 108-199). The act broadened the definition, keeping the population limit at 20,000, but eliminating the MSA prohibition, thereby permitting rural communities near large cities to receive loans. Thus the current definition used for rural communities is the same as what was used for the broadband pilot program, except that loans can now be issued to communities with preexisting service.

The definition of what constitutes a "rural" community is always a difficult issue for congressional policy makers in determining how to target rural communities for broadband

---

[43] Testimony of Jonathan Adelstein, Administrator of RUS, before the House Subcommittee on Communications and Technology, Committee on Energy and Commerce, April 1, 2011, p. 8, http://republicans.energycommerce house.gov/ Media/file/Hearings/Telecom/040111/Adelstein.pdf.

assistance. On the one hand, the narrower the definition the greater the possibility that deserving communities may be excluded. On the other hand, the broader the definition used, the greater the possibility that communities not traditionally considered "rural" or "underserved" may be eligible for financial assistance.

A related issue is the scope of coverage proposed by individual applications. While many of the loan applications propose broadband projects offering service to multiple rural communities, RUS identified a trend towards larger regional and national proposals, covering hundreds or even more than 1,000 communities.[44] The larger the scope of coverage, the greater the complexity of the loan application and the larger the possible benefits and risks to taxpayers.

Preexisting Broadband Service

Loans to areas with competitive preexisting service—that is, areas where existing companies already provide some level of broadband—sparked controversy because loan recipients are likely to compete with other companies already providing broadband service.

During reauthorization, Congress was asked to more sharply define whether and/or how loans should be given to companies serving rural areas with preexisting competitive service.[45] On the one hand, some argued that the federal government should not be subsidizing competitors for broadband service, particularly in sparsely populated rural markets which may be able only to support one provider. Furthermore, keeping communities with preexisting broadband service eligible may divert assistance from unserved areas that are most in need. On the other hand, many suburban and urban areas currently receive the benefits of competition between broadband providers—competition which can potentially drive down prices while improving service and performance. It is therefore appropriate, others argued, that rural areas also receive the benefits of competition, which in some areas may not be possible without federal financial assistance. It was also argued that it may not be economically feasible for borrowers to serve sparsely populated unserved communities unless they are permitted to also serve more lucrative areas which may already have existing providers.

Technological Neutrality

The 2002 farm bill (P.L. 107-171) directed RUS to use criteria that are "technologically neutral" in determining which projects to approve for loans. In other words, RUS is prohibited from typically valuing one broadband technology over another when assessing loan applications. As of November 10, 2008, 37% of approved and funded projects employed fiber-to-the-home technology, 17% employed DSL, 25% fixed wireless, 19% hybrid fiber-coaxial (cable), and 2% broadband over powerlines (BPL).[46] No funding has been provided for projects utilizing satellite broadband.[47]

---

[44] Rural Utilities Service, private communication, January 18, 2007.

[45] The statute (7 U.S.C. 950bb) allows States and local governments to be eligible for loans only if "no other eligible entity is already offering, or has committed to offer, broadband services to the eligible rural community."

[46] USDA, Rural Utilities Service, "FCC/USDA Rural Broadband Educational Workshop," power point presentation, November 20, 2008, http://www.usda.gov/rus/telecom/broadband/workshops/ FCC_USDABroadbandWorkshopNov20.pdf.

[47] According to the GAO, satellite companies state that RUS's broadband loan program requirements "are not readily (continued...)

While decisions on funded projects were required to be technologically neutral, RUS (through the Secretary of Agriculture) had the latitude to determine minimum required data transmission rates for broadband projects eligible for funding. According to the statute, "the Secretary shall, from time to time as advances in technology warrant, review and recommend modifications of rate-of-data transmission criteria for purposes of the identification of broadband service technologies."

Some argued that the minimum speed thresholds should be raised to ensure that rural areas receive "next-generation" broadband technologies with faster data rates capable of more varied and sophisticated applications. On the other hand, significantly raising minimum data rates could exclude certain technologies—for example typical data transmission rates for fiber and some wireless technologies exceed what is offered by "current generation" technologies such as DSL and cable. Proponents of keeping the minimum threshold at a low level argued that underserved rural areas are best served by any broadband technology that is economically feasible to deploy, regardless of whether it is "next" or "current" generation.

P.L. 110-246

The Food, Conservation, and Energy Act of 2008 became law on June 18, 2008 (P.L. 110-246). Section 6110, "Access to Broadband Telecommunications Services in Rural Areas," reauthorized the RUS broadband loan and loan guarantee program and addressed many of the criticisms and issues raised during the reauthorization process. The following summarizes broadband-related provisions that changed previous law.

Eligibility and Selection Criteria

- Defines rural area as any area other than (1) a city or town that has a population of greater than 20,000 and (2) an urbanized area contiguous and adjacent to a city or town with a population greater than 50,000. The Secretary may, by regulation only, consider not to be rural an area that consists of any collection of census blocks contiguous to each other with a housing density of more than 200 housing units per square mile and that is contiguous with or adjacent to an existing boundary of a rural area.

- Provides that the highest priority is to be given to applicants that offer to provide broadband service to the greatest proportion of households currently without broadband service. Eligible entities are required to submit a proposal to the Secretary that meets the requirements for a project to offer to provide service to a rural area and agree to complete build out of the broadband service within three years.

(...continued)

compatible with their business model or technology," and that "because the agency requires collateral for loans, the program is more suited for situations where the providers, rather than individual consumers, own the equipment being purchased through the loan. Yet, when consumers purchase satellite broadband, it is common for them to purchase the equipment needed to receive the satellite signal, such as the reception dish." Satellite companies argue that in some rural areas, satellite broadband might be the most feasible and cost-effective solution. See GAO, *Broadband Deployment is Extensive throughout the United States, but It Is Difficult to Assess the Extent of Deployment Gaps in Rural Areas*, pp. 34-35.

- Prohibits any eligible entity that provides telecommunications or broadband service to at least 20% of the households in the United States from receiving an amount of funds under this section for a fiscal year in excess of 15% of the funds authorized and appropriated for the broadband loan program.

- Directs the Secretary of Agriculture "from time to time as advances in technology warrant," to review and recommend modifications in rate-of-data transmission criteria for the purpose of identifying eligible broadband service technologies. At the same time, the Secretary is prohibited from establishing requirements for bandwidth or speed that have the effect of precluding the use of evolving technologies appropriate for use in rural areas.

Loans to Communities With Existing Providers

- Prohibits the Secretary from making a loan in any area where there are three or more incumbent service providers unless the loan meets all of the following requirements: (1) the loan is to an incumbent service provider that is upgrading service in that provider's existing territory; (2) the loan proposes to serve an area where not less than 25% of the households are offered service by not more than 1 provider; and (3) the applicant is not eligible for funding under another provision of the Rural Electrification Act. Incumbent service provider is defined as an entity providing broadband service to not less than 5% of the households in the service territory proposed in the application. Also prohibits the Secretary from making a loan in any area where not less than 25% of the households are offered broadband service by not more than one provider unless a prior loan has been made in the same area.

Financial Requirements

- Directs the Secretary to consider existing recurring revenues at the time of application in determining an adequate level of credit support. Requires the Secretary to ensure that the type, amount, and method of security used to secure a loan or loan guarantee is commensurate to the risk involved with the loan or loan guarantee, particularly when the loan or loan guarantee is issued to a financially healthy, strong, and stable entity. The Secretary is also required, in determining the amount and method of security, to consider reducing the security in areas that do not have broadband service.

- Allows the Secretary to require an entity to provide a cost-share in an amount not to exceed 10% of the amount of the loan or loan guarantee.

- Retains the current law rate of interest for direct loans—which is the rate equivalent to the cost of borrowing to the Department of Treasury for obligations of comparable maturity or 4%.

- Directs that loan or loan guarantee may have a term not to exceed 35 years if the Secretary determines that the loan security is sufficient.

- In case of substantially underserved trust areas (for example, Indian lands), where the Secretary determines a high need exists for the benefits of the program, the Secretary has the authority to provide loans with interest rates as low as 2%

and may waive nonduplication restrictions, matching fund requirements, credit support requirements, or other regulations.

Loan Application Requirements

- Allows the Secretary to require an entity that proposes to have a subscriber projection of more than 20% of the broadband service market in a rural area to submit a market survey. However, the Secretary is prohibited from requiring a market survey from an entity that projects to have less than 20% of the broadband market.

- Requires public notice of each application submitted, including the identity of the applicant, the proposed area to be served, and the estimated number of households in the application without terrestrial-based broadband. Authorizes the Secretary to take steps to reduce the costs and paperwork associated with applying for a loan or loan guarantee under this section by first-time applicants, particularly those who are smaller and start-up Internet providers.

- Allows the Secretary to establish a pre-application process under which a prospective applicant may seek a determination of area eligibility. Provides that an application, or a petition for reconsideration of a decision on such an application, that was pending on the date 45 days before enactment of this act and that remains pending on the date of enactment of this act is to be considered under eligibility and feasibility criteria in effect on the original date of submission of the application.

Other Provisions

- Authorizes the Rural Broadband Access Loan and Loan Guarantee program at $25 million to be appropriated for each of fiscal years 2008 through 2012.

- Requires that the Secretary annually report to Congress on the rural broadband loan and loan guarantee program. The annual report is to include information pertaining to the loans made, communities served and proposed to be served, speed of broadband service offered, types of services offered by the applicants and recipients, length of time to approve applications submitted, and outreach efforts undertaken by USDA.

- Section 6111 provides for a National Center for Rural Telecommunications Assessment. The Center is to assess the effectiveness of broadband loan programs, work with existing rural development centers to identify appropriate policy initiatives, and provide an annual report that describes the activities of the Center, the results of research carried out by the Center, and any additional information that the Secretary may request. An appropriation of $1 million is authorized for each of the fiscal years 2008 through 2012.

- Section 6112 directs the Chairman of the Federal Communications Commission (FCC), in coordination with the Secretary, to submit to Congress a report describing a comprehensive rural broadband strategy. Requires the report to be updated during the third year after enactment.

Implementation of P.L. 110-246

During 2009 and 2010, the Farm Bill Broadband Loan Program was on hiatus as RUS implemented the Broadband Initiatives Program (BIP) established under the American Recovery and Reinvestment Act of 2009 (P.L. 111-5). At the same time, final regulations implementing the broadband loan program as reauthorized by the 2008 farm bill were on hold and were being refined to reflect, in part, RUS experience in implementing BIP. Subsequently, on March 14, 2011, an Interim Rule and Notice was published in the *Federal Register* setting forth the rules and regulations for the broadband loan program as reauthorized by P.L. 110-246.[48] While the rule is immediately effective, RUS is accepting public comment before ultimately releasing a final rule. The application guide and all supporting materials for the Farm Bill Broadband Loan Program are available at http://www.rurdev.usda.gov/utp_farmbill.html.

Meanwhile, pursuant to Section 6112 of P.L. 110-246, the FCC released on May 22, 2009, its report on rural broadband strategy, entitled *Bringing Broadband to Rural America*.[49] The report made a series of recommendations including improved coordination of rural broadband efforts among federal agencies, states, and communities; better assessment of broadband needs, including technological considerations and broadband mapping and data; and overcoming challenges to rural broadband deployment.

Broadband Program Reauthorization: 2012 Farm Bill

As reauthorized by the 2008 farm bill, the Rural Broadband Access Loan and Loan Guarantee Program was authorized through FY2012. On April 26, 2012, the Senate Committee on Agriculture, Nutrition, and Forestry approved the Agriculture Reform, Food and Jobs Act of 2012 (S. 3240). Section 6104 of the act (Title VI, Rural Development) would have extended the RUS broadband program through FY2017. On June 20, 2012, the Senate agreed to amendment S.Amdt. 2457, offered by Senator Warner, that substituted an amended version of Section 6104. S. 3240 passed the Senate on June 21, 2012.

On April 25, 2012, the House Subcommittee on Rural Development, Research, Biotechnology, and Foreign Agriculture, Committee on Agriculture, held a hearing entitled, "Formulation of the 2012 Farm Bill: Rural Development Programs." Among those testifying were two witnesses representing the National Telecommunications Cooperative Association (NTCA), Organization for the Promotion and Advancement of Small Telecommunications Companies (OPASTCO), Western Telecommunications Alliance (WTA), and the National Cable and Telecommunications Association (NCTA).[50] Among the issues debated at the hearing was whether or not the rural broadband loan program should be modified to prohibit loans to projects serving areas with incumbent broadband service providers.

On July 9, 2012, H.R. 6083, the Federal Agriculture Reform and Risk Management Act of 2012 (FARRM), was introduced by Representative Lucas. Section 6105 of the act (Access to

---

[48] U.S. Department of Agriculture, Rural Utilities Service, "7 CFR Part 1738, Rural Broadband Access Loans and Loan Guarantees," 76 *Federal Register* 13770-13796, March 14, 2011.

[49] Michael J. Copps, Acting Chairman, Federal Communications Commission, *Bringing Broadband to Rural America: Report on a Rural Broadband Strategy*, May 22, 2009, 83 p.

[50] Hearing testimony is available at http://agriculture.house.gov/hearings/hearingDetails.aspx?NewsID=1567.

Broadband Telecommunications Services in Rural Areas) would have amended the current broadband statute (Section 601 of the Rural Electrification Act of 1936 (7 U.S.C. 950bb)).

H.R. 6083 was marked up by the House Committee on Agriculture and approved on July 12, 2012. During the July 11 markup, the committee adopted an amendment offered by Representative Johnson of Illinois that instructs the Secretary to give priority to applicants that offer to provide broadband service not predominantly for business service, but where at least 25% of customers in the proposed service territory are commercial interests. The committee rejected an amendment offered by Representative Gibson that would have authorized loan-grant combinations.

The 2012 farm bill (S. 3240/H.R. 6083) was ultimately not enacted by the 112th Congress. However, Title VII of the American Taxpayer Relief Act of 2012 extended farm bill program authorizations, including the broadband program, by one year (through September 30, 2013).

Meanwhile, other introduced bills, relating to the 2012 farm bill broadband program, included the following:

- S. 1895, the Upstate Works Act introduced by Senator Gillibrand on November 17, 2011, would have extended the Farm Bill broadband loan program authorization through FY2017.

- S. 2275, the Broadband Connections for Rural Opportunities Program (BCROP) Act of 2012 introduced by Senator Gillibrand on March 29, 2012, would have amended the Rural Electrification Act to establish a broadband grant program, define an eligible rural area as under 50,000 population, provide refinements to the application process, establish a rural broadband clearinghouse website, and require reports to Congress on the effectiveness of all federal broadband assistance programs and policies.

- S. 2298, the Connecting Rural America Act introduced by Senator Brown of Ohio on April 18, 2012, would have amended the Rural Electrification Act to establish a broadband grant program, set the definition of an incumbent service provider as serving no less than 15% of the households in a service area (up from 5% in the current statute), establish transparency and reporting requirements, provide mandatory annual funding of $20 million from the Commodity Credit Corporation, and in addition to funds otherwise made available, authorize $25 million in annual appropriations through FY2017.

Broadband Program Reauthorization: 2013 and 2014 Farm Bills

In the 113th Congress, 2013 farm bill legislation in the House and Senate includes the broadband program reauthorization provisions contained in the 2012 farm bill. Both the House and Senate bills would extend the reauthorization of the RUS broadband program through FY2018.

Senate Bill, S. 954

On May 14, 2013, the Senate Committee on Agriculture, Nutrition, and Forestry reported the Agriculture Reform, Food and Jobs Act of 2013 (S. 954, introduced by Senator Stabenow). S. 954 was passed by the Senate on June 10, 2013. The Senate adopted S.Amdt. 998 (introduced by Senator Leahy), which expands pilot loan and grant projects to include ultra-high speed service (1 gigabit per second or higher downstream speeds). Section 6104 of S. 954 ("Access to Broadband Telecommunications Services in Rural Areas"), as passed by the Senate, includes the following changes from the broadband provision in the current statute (7 U.S.C. 950bb):

- Broadband grants—A new broadband grant program is added to the existing loan and loan guarantee program authorization. The bill specifies that the amount of any grant shall not exceed 50% of the development costs of the grant projects (e.g., 50% is set as the maximum federal cost share rate). However, the USDA Secretary has the authority to adjust that rate up to 75% if it is determined that the project serves a remote or low income area that does not have access to broadband service from any provider.

- Definition of rural area—Under S. 954, all rural development programs, including the broadband grant and loan program, would conform to a uniform definition of a rural area: any area that is not a city or town with a population greater than 50,000, and that is not an urbanized area contiguous and adjacent to a city or town with a population over 50,000. Because the current definition of a rural area eligible for broadband loans is towns with populations under 20,000, this new definition would increase the number of communities eligible for broadband assistance.

- Definition of broadband service—S. 954 establishes "the minimum acceptable level of broadband service" as at least 4 Mbps downstream and 1 Mbps upstream. At least once every two years, the Secretary may adjust this speed definition and may consider establishing different minimum speeds for fixed and mobile (wireless) broadband. The current statute states that from "time to time" the Secretary shall recommend modifications in speed criteria for broadband.

- Project area eligibility—S. 954 lowers the maximum allowable number of incumbent providers in any part of an eligible service area from two to one. Additionally, S. 954 provides that an eligible area is one where no less than 25% of the households in the proposed service territory are unserved or have broadband service levels below the minimum acceptable level of broadband service (which is set at 4 Mbps/1 Mbps). Current statute states that eligible areas must (with some exceptions) have not more than one incumbent broadband provider in not less than 25% of households in the proposed service area. S. 3240 allows RUS to increase the 25% requirement if more than 25% of the project cost is being funded by a grant, or if there is one or more communities in the proposed service area with populations over 20,000. RUS can decrease the 25% requirement to 18% for service areas with a population less than 7,500, and to 15% for populations under 5,000.

- Evaluation period—S. 954 directs RUS to establish not less than two, and not more than four, evaluation periods for each fiscal year to compare and prioritize grant, loan, and loan guarantee applications. Under current statute, broadband loan applications are submitted and considered year-round—there is no set application or evaluation period.

- Priority setting—S. 954 directs RUS to give the highest priority to applicants that offer to provide broadband service to the greatest proportion of unserved rural households or rural households that do not have residential broadband service that meets the minimum acceptable level of broadband service, as certified by the affected community, city, county, or designee; or demonstrated on the broadband map of the affected state if the map contains address-level data, or the National Broadband Map if address-level data are unavailable. RUS shall provide equal consideration to all qualified applicants, including those that have not previously received grants, loans, or loan guarantees. After giving priority to the applicants described above, RUS shall then give priority to projects that serve rural communities with a population of less than 20,000, with a high percentage of low-income residents, that are isolated from other significant population centers, and that are experiencing outmigration. Current statute directs RUS to give highest priority to applicants that offer to provide broadband service to the greatest proportion of households that, prior to the provision of the broadband service, had no incumbent service provider.

- Transparency—RUS shall promptly post on its website an announcement that identifies each applicant; the amount and type of support requested by each applicant; and a list of the census block groups that the applicant proposes to service. RUS will provide not less than 15 days for broadband service providers to voluntarily submit information about the broadband services that the providers offer in the groups or tracts listed so that RUS may assess whether the applications submitted meet the eligibility requirements. If no broadband service provider submits this information, RUS will consider the number of providers in the group or tract to be established by reference to the most current National Broadband Map or any other data RUS may collect or obtain through reasonable efforts. Current statute requires that RUS publish a notice of each application, including the identity of the applicant, each area proposed to be served by the applicant, and the estimated number of households without terrestrial-based broadband service in those areas.

- Recipient and applicant reporting—The Secretary shall require quarterly reports from grant and loan recipients describing in detail the use of the assistance, and the progress towards fulfilling project objectives. RUS shall maintain a fully searchable database on the Internet that contains a list of each entity that has applied for assistance, and the description status of each application. For each entity receiving assistance, the database shall provide the name of the entity, the type of assistance being received, the purpose for which the entity is receiving the assistance, and each quarterly report submitted. There is no requirement in current statute for quarterly reports or for RUS to post such information on the Internet.

- De-obligation—S. 954 directs RUS to establish written procedures for recovering funds from loan defaults, de-obligating awards to grantees that demonstrate an insufficient level of performance or wasteful or fraudulent spending, awarding those funds to new or existing applicants, and consolidating and minimizing overlap among programs. There is no comparable language in the current statute.

- Report to Congress—S. 954 adds requirements to the content of the annual report to Congress, including the number of residences and businesses receiving new broadband services; network improvements, including facility upgrades and equipment purchases; average broadband speeds and prices on a local and statewide basis; any changes in broadband adoption rates; and any specific activities that increase high speed broadband access for educational institutions, health care providers, and public safety service providers.

- Broadband build-out data—As a condition of receiving a grant, loan, or loan guarantee, a recipient shall provide to RUS address-level broadband build-out data that indicate the location of new broadband service that is being provided or upgraded within the service territory supported. These data will be included in the semiannual updates to the National Telecommunications and Information Administration's (NTIA's) National Broadband Map, and effective beginning on the date NTIA receives the data, NTIA shall use only address-level broadband build-out data for the National Broadband Map. RUS shall submit to NTIA any correction to the National Broadband Map that is based on the actual level of broadband coverage within the rural area, including any requests for a correction from an elected or economic development official. Not later than 30 days after the date on which the NTIA receives a correction submitted, NTIA shall incorporate the correction into the National Broadband Map. There is no comparable provision in current statute.

- Pilot programs—The Secretary may carry out pilot programs in conjunction with state and local governments and Indian tribes (which may be in partnership with other entities, as determined appropriate by the Secretary) to address areas that are unserved or have service levels below the minimum acceptable level of broadband service, or to provide a limited number of projects offering ultra-high speed service, defined as downstream speeds of 1 gigabit per second or higher. There is no comparable provision in the statute.

- Market survey requirement—S. 954 provides that survey information must be certified by the affected community, city, county, or designee; and demonstrated on the broadband map of the affected state if the map contains address-level data, or the National Broadband Map if address-level data are unavailable. The current statute has no such requirement for certification and demonstration of market survey information.

- Terms and conditions—In determining the term and conditions of assistance, the Secretary may consider whether the recipient would be serving an area that is unserved, and if so, can establish a limited initial deferral period or comparable terms necessary to achieve the financial feasibility and long-term sustainability of the project. There is no such deferral period authorized in the current statute.

- Authorization S. 954 authorizes the broadband grant, loan, and loan guarantee program at $50 million per year through FY2018, with at least 1% to be used for conducting oversight and implementing the accountability measures and related activities authorized. S. 3240 does not specify how the authorized amount should be divided between grants, loans, and loan guarantees. The current statute authorized the loan and loan guarantee program at $25 million per year through FY2012, and did not set aside funding for administrative purposes.

House Bill, H.R. 2642

H.R. 2642, the Federal Agriculture Reform and Risk Management Act of 2013 (FARRM), was passed by the House on July 11, 2013. Section 5106 of H.R. 2642 ("Access to Broadband Telecommunications Services in Rural Areas") would make the following changes to the current broadband loan statute:

- while continuing to provide that the highest priority is to be given applicants that "offer to provide broadband service to the greatest proportion of households that, prior to the provision of broadband service had no incumbent service provider," H.R. 2642 additionally instructs the Secretary to give priority to applicants that offer to provide broadband service not predominantly for business service, but where at least 25% of customers in the proposed service territory are commercial interests;

- instructs the Secretary to include additional information in its public notice of each loan application, including the amount and type of support requested, and a list of the census block groups or tracts proposed to be served;

- requires the Secretary to establish a process under which an incumbent service provider may (but shall not be required to) submit not less than 15 days and not more than 30 days after the publication of the public notice, information regarding the broadband services that the provider offers in the proposed service territory, so that the Secretary may assess whether the application meets the eligibility requirements;

- in considering the technology needs of customers in a proposed service territory, the Secretary is directed to take into consideration the upgrade or replacement cost for the construction or acquisition of facilities and equipment in the territory; and

- reauthorizes the broadband loan and loan guarantee program through FY2018 at the current level of $25 million per year.

P.L. 113-79, the Agricultural Act of 2014

On January 27, 2014, the conference report for the Agricultural Act of 2014 was filed (H.Rept. 113-333). The conference agreement was approved by the House on January 29, approved by the Senate on February 4, and signed into law (P.L. 113-79) by the President on February 7, 2014.

P.L. 113-79 amends Section 601 of the Rural Electrification Act of 1936 (7 U.S.C. 950bb) to reauthorize the Rural Broadband Access Loan and Loan Guarantee Program through FY2018. P.L. 113-79 also includes provisions to redefine project area eligibility with respect to existing broadband service, increase the program's transparency and reporting requirements, define a minimum level of broadband service, require a study on the gathering and use of address-level data, and establish a new Rural Gigabit Network Pilot Program. The conference agreement did **not** include the Senate bill proposal to create a new grant component to the existing broadband loan and loan guarantee program, nor did the conference agreement adopt the Senate bill's broadening of the definition for eligible rural areas.

Specifically, Section 6104 of P.L. 113-79 makes the following changes to the Rural Broadband Access Loan and Loan Guarantee program:

- Project area eligibility—provides that an eligible area is one where not less than 15% of the households in the proposed service territory are unserved or have service levels below the minimum acceptable level of broadband service (which is set at 4 Mbps/1 Mbps).

- Priority—directs RUS to give the highest priority to applicants that offer to provide broadband service to the greatest proportion of unserved households or households that do not have residential broadband service that meets the minimum acceptable level of broadband service, as certified by the affected community, city, county, or designee; or demonstrated on the broadband map of the affected state if the map contains address-level data, or the National Broadband Map if address-level data are unavailable. RUS shall provide equal consideration to all qualified applicants, including those that have not previously received grants, loans, or loan guarantees. Also gives priority to applicants that offer to provide broadband service not predominantly for business service, but if at least 25% of customers in the proposed service territory are commercial interests

- Evaluation period—directs RUS to establish not less than two evaluation periods for each fiscal year to compare loan and loan guarantee applications and to prioritize loans and loan guarantees to all or part of rural communities that do not have residential broadband service that meets the minimum acceptable level of broadband service.

- Market survey requirement—provides that survey information must be certified by the affected community, city, county, or designee; and demonstrated on the broadband map of the affected state if the map contains address-level data, or the National Broadband Map if address-level data are unavailable.

- Notice requirement—directs RUS to maintain a fully searchable database on the Internet that contains a list of each entity that has applied for assistance, the status of each application, and a detailed description of each application. For each entity receiving assistance, the database shall provide the name of the entity, the type of assistance being received, the purpose for which the entity is receiving the assistance, and each semiannual report submitted.

- Reporting—requires semiannual reports from loan recipients for three years after completion of the project describing in detail the use of the assistance, and the progress towards fulfilling project objectives.

- Default and deobligation—directs RUS to establish written procedures for recovering funds from loan defaults, deobligating awards that demonstrate an insufficient level of performance or fraudulent spending, awarding those funds to new or existing applicants, and minimizing overlap among programs.

- Service area assessment—directs RUS to promptly post on its website a list of the census block groups that an applicant proposes to service. RUS will provide not less than 15 days for broadband service providers to voluntarily submit information about the broadband services that the providers offer in the groups or tracts listed so that RUS may assess whether the applications submitted meet the eligibility requirements. If no broadband service provider submits this information, RUS will consider the number of providers in the group or tract to be established by reference to the most current National Broadband Map or any other data RUS may collect or obtain through reasonable efforts.

- Definition of broadband service—establishes "the minimum acceptable level of broadband service" as at least 4 Mbps downstream and 1 Mbps upstream. At least once every two years, the Secretary shall review and may adjust this speed definition and may consider establishing different minimum speeds for fixed and mobile (wireless) broadband.

- Terms and conditions—in determining the terms and conditions of assistance, the Secretary may consider whether the recipient would be serving an area that is unserved (or has service levels below the minimum acceptable level of broadband service), and if so, can establish a limited initial deferral period or comparable terms necessary to achieve the financial feasibility and long-term sustainability of the project.

- Report to Congress—adds requirements to the content of the annual report to Congress, including the number of residences and businesses receiving new broadband services; network improvements, including facility upgrades and equipment purchases; average broadband speeds and prices on a local and statewide basis; any changes in broadband adoption rates; and any specific activities that increase high speed broadband access for educational institutions, health care providers, and public safety service providers.

- Reauthorization—reauthorizes the broadband loan and loan guarantee program through FY2018 at the current level of $25 million per year.

- Study on providing effective data for the National Broadband Map—directs USDA, in consultation with DOC and the FCC, to conduct a study of the ways data collected by RUS could most effectively be shared with the FCC to support the development and maintenance of the National Broadband Map. The study shall include a consideration of the circumstances under which address-level data could be collected by RUS and appropriately shared with the FCC.

Additionally, Section 6105 establishes a new Rural Gigabit Network Pilot Program. Specifically, USDA is authorized to provide grants, loans, or loan guarantees for projects that would extend ultra-high speed broadband service (defined as 1 gigabit per second downstream capacity) to rural areas where ultra-high speed service is not provided in any part of the proposed service territory. The pilot program is authorized at $10 million per year for the years FY2014 through FY2018.

Author Contact Information

Lennard G. Kruger
Specialist in Science and Technology Policy
lkruger@crs.loc.gov, 7-7070